CHARLES T. GRIFFES

THE PLEASURE-DOME OF KUBLA KHAN

Piano Solo

Edited by Donna K. Anderson

ED-3852
First printing: June 1993

G. SCHIRMER, Inc.

DISTRIBUTED BY
HAL•LEONARD®
CORPORATION
7777 W. BLUEMOUND RD. P.O. BOX 13819 MILWAUKEE, WI 53213

One of Charles T. Griffes' best-known works is his exotic and exquisitely colored orchestral tone-poem, *The Pleasure-Dome of Kubla Khan*. When Pierre Monteux and the Boston Symphony Orchestra premiered the work in Boston in November 1919 and repeated it in New York in December during their Carnegie Hall series, Griffes seemed to appear on the musical scene like a meteor. In reality, he had been steadily and successfully building a career since 1909, the year G. Schirmer published five German songs, the first of Griffes' works to appear in print. Especially from 1915 on, Griffes' name began to appear with regularity in New York newspapers and in music periodicals such as *Musical America* and *Musical Courier*. There is no question, however, that the *Pleasure-Dome* performances were an important milestone in Griffes' career, perhaps *the* most important. They resulted in critical acclaim and attention far beyond Griffes' wildest dreams. He was lauded as one of the most gifted composers ever produced in America, a composer of individuality and imagination. More than one critic remarked on the promise of things to come from Griffes, but, tragically, the composer died on April 8, 1920, just a few months after the *Pleasure-Dome* premiere.

What many people do not realize is that *The Pleasure-Dome of Kubla Khan* was first written as a piano composition. Griffes began the piano version sometime before March 11, 1912 (when he mentioned in his diary that he had worked some on it that day), continued to work on it, remarking on September 23, that he had never "changed and changed a piece" as much as he had the *Pleasure-Dome*. In November 1912, Griffes played the *Pleasure-Dome* for pianist Gottfried Galston, with whom he had studied piano in Germany, and Galston told him that he thought the composition was essentially an orchestral piece. In 1915, Griffes was still working on the composition, noting in his diary on February 6, "Have changed and simplified it again. It improves every time." On March 11, 1915, Griffes played the piece for the composer-pianist Ferruccio Busoni, who advised Griffes to either shorten the piano version, or re-do the piece for orchestra. On December 5, 1915 Griffes wrote in his diary, "Worked a good deal on a new version of 'Kubla Khan' which I may fix up for orchestra." Griffes probably arrived at a final version of the piano piece in 1915. He then did, indeed, "fix up" a version of *The Pleasure-Dome of Kubla Khan* for orchestra (really a metamorphosis, not just a simple orchestration) between February 1916 and late 1917.

Three manuscripts of the piano version of *The Pleasure-Dome of Kubla Khan* are extant, all housed in The New York Public Library. One is in sketch form (probably his first version), and the other two are complete fair copies, both titled and signed by Griffes (one manuscript is dated 1912). The latter two manuscripts are similar in many respects: the version dated 1912 is slightly longer and contains fewer expression marks, pedal indications, and fingerings than the undated fair copy. The score, being published for the first time by G. Schirmer, is a combination of Griffes' two fair copy manuscripts. It was first performed by pianist James Tocco on September 21, 1984 in Coolidge Auditorium, the Library of Congress, Washington, D.C. Mr. Tocco has also recorded the work for Gasparo Records (GSCD-234).

—DONNA K. ANDERSON

duration: ca. 10 minutes

Performance material (for the orchestral version) is available on rental from the publisher.

THE PLEASURE-DOME OF KUBLA KHAN

Charles T. Griffes

Edited by Donna K. Anderson

poco a poco più mosso

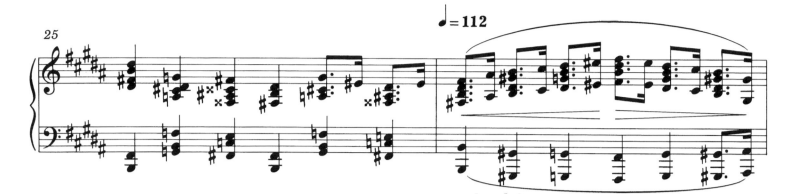

col pedale

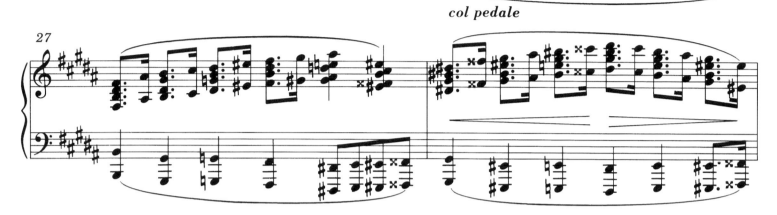

crescendo

8va -

(8) -

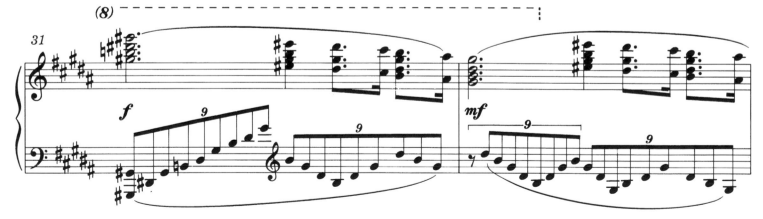

poco ritenuto

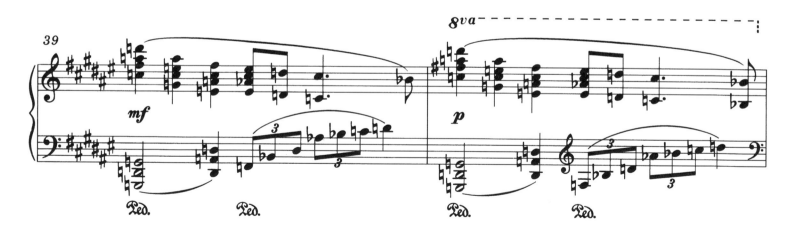

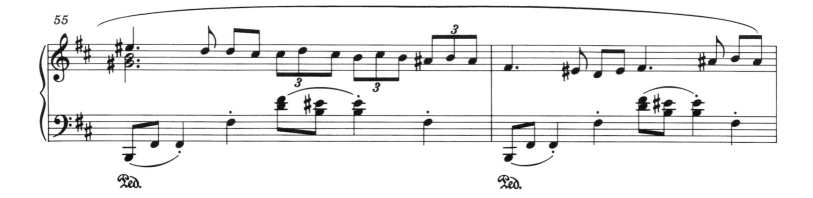

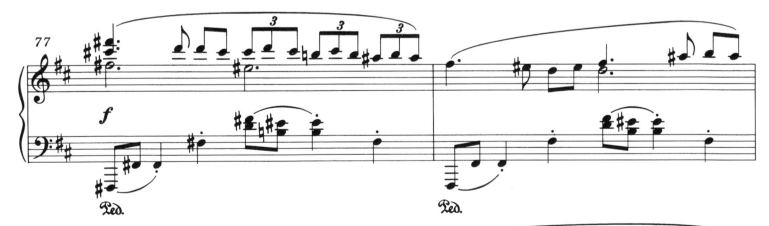

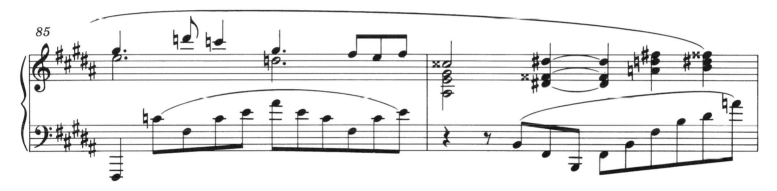

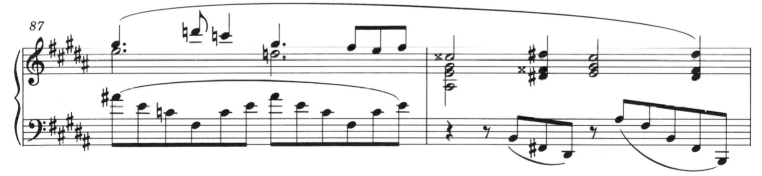

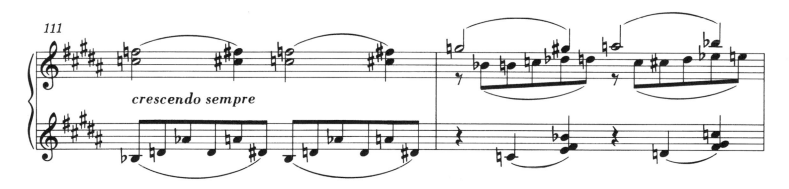

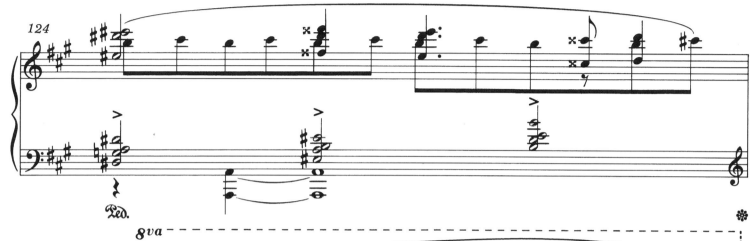

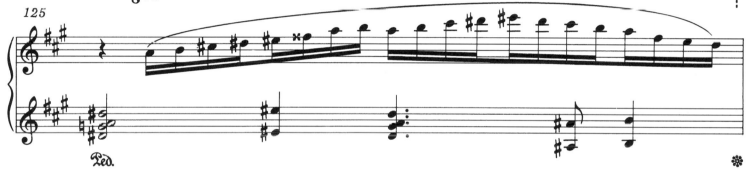

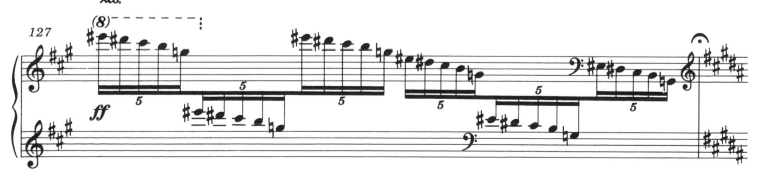

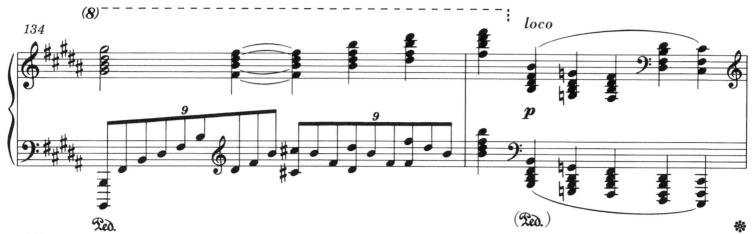

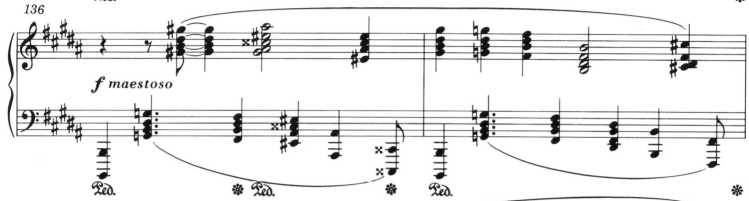

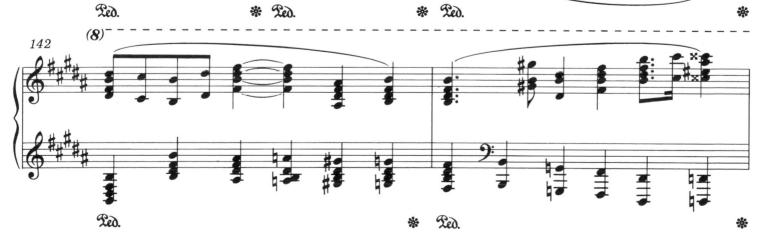

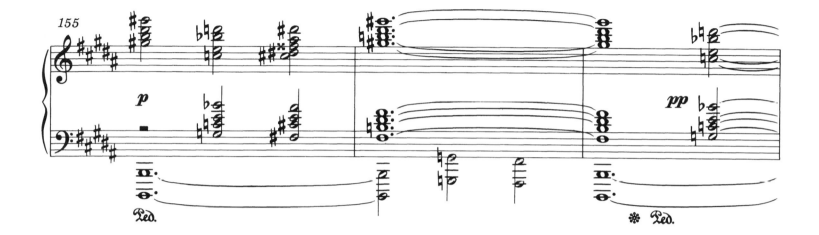

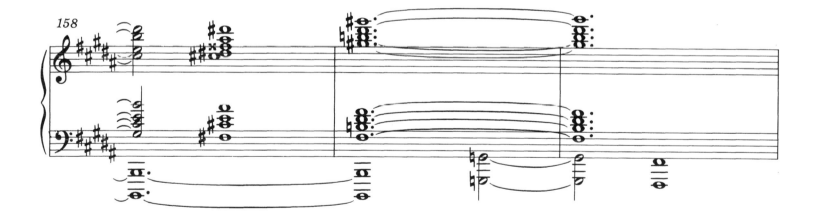

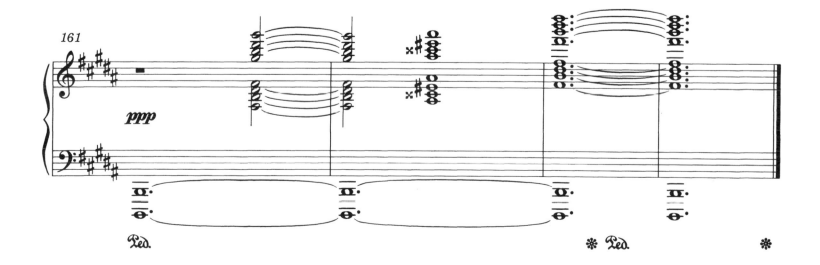